Marinated Peri Chicken Thighs and Drumsticks ... Page 34

VEGETARIAN

66

ONE-POT

82

DESSERTS

96

D1359949

3

Introduction

Jean Patrique has been making professional cookware for over 21 years. Over time, our product range has grown, along with our customer base. Every year we receive thousands of requests for new products from our customers, however, the most frequently requested product in 2020 was not a new piece of kitchenware, a pan, or a knife.

It was, in fact, the very cookbook you are holding. With the success and popularity of the Whatever Pan, our customers asked us to bring together all of our best recipes, and food inspiration into a book they could own. And here it is! The very first edition, and Jean Patrique's debut into the publishing world.

The recipes in this book are just as versatile as the Whatever Pan itself. You'll find a wide variety of delicious meat and seafood dishes, tasty vegetarian options, simple one-pot meals and plenty of delightful desserts. We guarantee this book will inspire your inner chef and get you grilling, searing and baking like a pro.

We've partnered with some brilliant chefs to develop delicious yet uncomplicated recipes for all occasions. Whether you're looking for quick ideas for dinner (White Fish Tagine), craving something comforting at the end of a long week, (One Skillet Lasagne) or want to indulge in a decadent dessert (Caramel-Pecan Cheesecake), the recipes in this book are sure to become firm favourites.

You don't have to rely on the book alone, each recipe has a unique QR code, simply scan this with your smartphone and follow the link to watch a video tutorial. As a bonus, we've included a handy guide on how to care for your Whatever Pan (page 106) once you've finished every last delicious morsel!

Meet the Chefs

Each of our collaborating chefs has contributed their unique flavours and culinary experiences to the recipes in this cookbook.

Luca La Rosa

 @tokitchen_torino

"I'm a professional chef based in Turin, Italy. I own and run two restaurants specialising in authentic Italian Cuisine and Mediterranean Flavours. I've served tens of thousands of customers in my restaurants including renowned food critics. I also work as a food and beverage consultant, and in my spare time I love to teach students the secrets of Italian cuisine.

I've developed simple but impactful recipes for this cookbook that I'm sure you will master - all you need is curiosity and a love of food!"

Layla Powell

 @laylayskitchen

"Food and cooking have always been a constant joy for me. In my later years, it's become my form of meditation. I grew up in the UK within a mixed Caribbean and North African family that gifted me an immense amount of cultural richness in the kitchen. We have always had exotic spices and mouth-watering hearty dishes that have influenced my style of cooking today.

Eating well and healthy at home is something that I feel strongly about, and I convey this feeling with dishes that feel like home-cooked Extravaganzas."

Inocan Ákos

@akos616

"I started working as a chef in 2015. Having just moved to a new city in Romania, Cluj Napoca, I had no idea of what I really wanted to do with my life. I got a job in a restaurant as a dish washer and one day I cooked a meal for a customer. He liked it so much that I knew I was destined for more. I felt the calling voice of being a chef.

I believe that every recipe has its own soul and yours has to be in harmony with it."

Men with the Pot

@menwiththepot @menwiththepot

Slawek Kalkraut and Krzysztof Szymanski, aka Men With The Pot, cook delicious meals over open fires in the forests around Fermanagh, Northern Ireland where they live and work. During 2020 the incredible outdoor cooking videos they create went viral on TikTok which saw their following explode to over 4.4 million people with their most popular video hitting 37 million views alone. Many of their videos feature our very own Whatever Pan, and we've handpicked the best recipes for you to try yourself. But don't worry, you don't have to cook them outdoors over a fire, you can just as easily make them in your kitchen at home.

Ribeye Steak with Lemon Herbal Butter

This boneless rib-eye steak topped with lemon and herb butter = extra juicy indulgence.

 20 Mins · Serves 2

Ingredients

- 2 rib-eye steaks
- Salt
- Freshly ground pepper

For the butter compound:

- 120g/½ cup butter
- 20g/¼ cup herbs (parsley, thyme, rosemary)
- Zest of one lemon
- 2 cloves of garlic, minced

Method

1. Start by making the butter compound by mixing the butter with the herbs, zest of one lemon, and garlic and let chill for 15 minutes.

2. Preheat the Whatever Pan and drizzle your ribeye steaks with salt and pepper.

3. Once the pan is hot add your steaks and start frying away.

4. Cook until a dark crust has formed, for about 1 minute. Using a spatula, flip, and cook for an additional minute.

5. Add a spoonful of butter compound to both steaks and serve.

RECOMMENDED PRODUCT

BAMBOO SPATULA

Homemade Big Max Burger

Let's recreate one of our guilty pleasures usually obtained from the double arches. Make your own world famous burger at home. Yes, even the 'secret sauce' is revealed!

 30 Mins Serves 1

Ingredients

- 250g/½lb ground beef
- 1.5 burger buns
- 2 slices American cheese
- 1 gherkin
- Lettuce
- Salt and pepper, to taste

Burger sauce

- 105g/½ cup mayonnaise
- 15g/1 tbsp yellow mustard
- 15g/1 tbsp garlic powder
- 15g/1 tbsp onion powder
- 7g/1½ tsp white pepper
- 15g/1 tbsp smoked paprika
- 1 tbsp white vinegar

Method

1. Start by making your patties as thick as you like, then season with salt and pepper.

2. Then, toast your burger buns in the Whatever Pan on medium heat until one of the sides is golden brown.

3. Fry both patties for 2 and a half minutes a side and add a slice of cheese to each.

4. For the burger sauce mix: mayonnaise, yellow mustard, garlic powder, onion powder, white pepper, smoked paprika and white vinegar. Set aside.

5. Time to build this bad boy! Spread burger sauce on the bottom bun, sprinkle lettuce and gherkin. Add the patty with cheese and place another slice of bun.

6. Add more sauce, more shredded lettuce, gherkin slices, another patty and the last slice of bun.

Blue Cheese Burger

Salty blue cheese, sweet onions and juicy beef are a classic and addictive combination. A perfect summer burger!

 20 Mins Serves 2

Ingredients

- 2 tbsp. olive oil
- 1 onion, thinly sliced
- 1 tsp. kosher salt
- 1 lb. ground beef
- ½ tsp. freshly ground black pepper
- 3oz./85g bacon or two rashers
- 115g/4oz. blue cheese
- 2 Hamburger buns
- 2 tbsp. ketchup
- 2 tbsp. mayonnaise
- ½ tomato
- 1oz. or a generous handful of rocket salad

Method

1. In your Whatever Pan, add onion and olive oil and heat over medium heat.

2. Fry for a few minutes and let cool.

3. Add the onion to your ground beef and add salt and pepper. Then, mix well and shape into 2 patties.

4. Heat your Whatever Pan and add the patties and bacon. Cook for approximately 5 minutes, until the sides have a nice dark brown crust. Flip the patties and cook for another 5 minutes for medium done results.

5. Crumble the blue cheese over each patty, and cover with a lid until the cheese melts.

6. Meanwhile, prepare your buns. Add ketchup on a bun, and mayonnaise on the other.

7. Build your burgers! Add the bacon, patties, tomato slices and rocket.

8. Serve and enjoy!

Chili Con Carne

Spice up you life with this delicious Chili con carne recipe. Perfect for all Mexican food lovers!

 35 Mins Serves 4

Ingredients

- 225g/8oz bacon
- 450g/1lb minced beef
- 235ml/1 cup beef broth
- 85g/1 cup cheddar cheese
- Handful of fresh parsley
- 400g/1 can tomatoes
- 1 medium onion
- 3 garlic cloves
- ½ tsp dried thyme leaves
- 1 tsp chili pepper
- 1 tsp black pepper
- 1 tsp dried Mexican oregano
- 2 tsp paprika
- ½ tsp salt

Method

1. Heat your Whatever Pan and start frying the bacon. Add onion and garlic and cook until onion is golden.

2. Add the beef, chili pepper, black pepper, Mexican oregano, paprika, thyme leaves and salt and stir well.

3. Add all of the beef broth, the tomatoes, then cover with lid and stew for 2 hours.

4. Once cooked add the cheddar cheese and place in the oven.

5. Bake at 205°C/400°F for 10 minutes, sprinkle some parsley and serve!

Fillet Steak Flambe

If you're looking for something to cook for a special occasion, this recipe definitely has the wow factor. Flambéing adds a delicious depth of flavour.

 25 Mins   Serves 1

Ingredients

- Fillet steak, ideally 2.5cm thick
- ½ tbsp. butter
- Olive oil
- 1 tsp. mustard seeds
- 1 tsp. English mustard
- ¼ bell pepper, cut into thin strips
- Handful of chestnut mushrooms
- 100ml/3.5oz. Brandy
- 250ml/⅓ of bottle red wine
- 100ml/3.5oz. single cream
- Fresh parsley
- Salt and pepper, to taste

Method

1. Brush the fillet steak on both sides with olive oil, then season with salt and pepper.

2. Place your Whatever Pan on high heat. After heating, place the steak in the pan and cook for 6 minutes, turning regularly and making sure the edges are seared.

3. Meanwhile, toast mustard seeds in the pan. Then, add mustard, bell pepper, mushrooms and season with salt and pepper.

4. Pour in the Brandy, and carefully light with a long match to let it flambé – stand back! When the flames subside, add the red wine and reduce by half.

5. Add fresh parsley and pour in the cream.

6. Let this cook for a few minutes, then transfer onto a plate.

7. Cut your steak into chunks and place on the sauce. Pour the remaining sauce on the steak and serve!

Pork Chops with Balsamic Roasted Vegetables and Gorgonzola

A quick and super tasty recipe for all the meat and cheese lovers out there!

 60 Mins Serves 2

Ingredients

- 4 boneless centre-cut loin pork chops
- 340g/12 oz. small red potatoes
- Cremini mushrooms
- 1 red onion
- 1 tbsp gorgonzola
- 2 tbsp balsamic vinegar
- 2 tbsp tomato paste
- Fresh thyme
- Parsley
- Olive oil
- Kosher salt and black pepper, to taste

Method

1. Preheat oven 220°C/425°F.
2. Sprinkle ¼ tsp salt and pepper on both sides of the pork chops.
3. Heat the Whatever Pan on high heat and add 2 tbsp of olive oil. Add your pork chops and fry for 3 minutes per side.
4. Set aside and start frying your potatoes. Cook for 2 minutes and set aside.
5. In a small mixing bowl add ½ tsp black pepper, 2 tbsp olive oil, 2 tbsp of balsamic vinegar, and 2 tbsp tomato paste. Whisk well and set aside.
6. In a medium bowl add mushrooms, onion, 2 tbsp of your vinegar mixture, 1 tbsp of fresh thyme and mix well.
7. Add 1 tbsp of olive oil to a baking tray, add the potatoes and vegetables and place in the oven for 25 minutes. Stir every 10 minutes.
8. Remove from the oven, add your pork chops and bake for another 10 minutes.
9. Remove from the oven and place ingredients on a plate. Then, add your vinegar mixture, parsley, Gorgonzola and serve!

Roasted Veal Chop

Here's a healthy and nutritious meal that includes a side of generously seasoned vegetables, all cooked in the same pan! All the flavours and juices combined wonderfully to make a mouthwatering meal.

 45 Mins  Serves 1

Ingredients

- 2 tbsp of vegetable oil
- 1 tbsp white peppercorns
- 1 veal chop
- 1 tbsp paprika powder
- 1 tbsp butter
- 4 cloves of garlic
- Handful of mixed herbs
- 1 red pepper, cut into thick chunks
- 1 chilli pepper, sliced
- 6 cherry tomatoes, halved
- ½ red onion, sliced
- Salt, to taste

Method

1. Preheat the oven to 200°C/390°F.

2. Heat vegetable oil in your Whatever Pan and throw in the white peppercorns to infuse the oil.

3. Place the veal chop in the pan and sprinkle the paprika over it. Cook the veal chop for 2-3 minutes per side. After turning, season with salt.

4. Put the butter onto the veal chop, and let it melt in the Whatever Pan.

5. Throw in garlic cloves and fresh herbs and cook for a few minutes. Then, add the red pepper, chilli, tomatoes and red onion.

6. Pop it in the oven and roast for 20 minutes. Then, serve!

RECOMMENDED PRODUCT

BAMBOO SPOON

Citrus and Chile Braised Short Ribs

For all the meat lovers out there, here's a succulent ribs recipe that will definitely satisfy your appetite!

 20 Mins   Serves 2

Ingredients

- 1 tbsp vegetable oil
- 3 bone-in-beef short ribs
- 1 medium onion, finely chopped
- 1 medium carrot, chopped
- 2 celery stalks, chopped
- 2 tbsp tomato paste
- 1 tsp cumin seeds
- 1 tsp crushed red pepper flakes
- Salt and pepper to taste
- 1 tsp oregano
- 500ml/2 cups orange juice
- 3 strips orange zest
- 500ml/2 cups water
- Juice of ½ lime
- 2 strips orange zest for garnishing
- Fresh parsley to taste

Method

1. Preheat oven to 170°C/340°F and season your short ribs with salt and pepper.

2. Heat vegetable oil in your Whatever Pan and cook short ribs for about 5 minutes on each side, until evenly browned.

3. Set aside your short ribs. Remove any burned bits from the Whatever Pan but leave the golden-brown pieces (this will keep the sauce from tasting bitter).

4. Start frying the onion, carrots and celery. After a couple of minutes, add tomato paste, cumin seeds, red pepper flakes, salt, pepper and oregano and then stir. Increase the heat to medium-high and cook for about 10 minutes until the vegetables are softened.

5. Add 1 cup of orange juice, 3 strips of orange zest and water.

6. Add your short ribs back into the pan with the vegetables.

7. Cover with lid and braise ribs in the oven until the meat is tender, about 4 hours.

8. To serve, plate up the short ribs and vegetables and drizzle with remaining orange and lime juice, then garnish with orange zest and parsley.

Beef fillet
Mediterranean style

This beef dish is bursting with flavour and complexity but is simple and quick to prepare.

 40 Mins   Serves 2

Ingredients

- 250g/½ lb beef fillet
- 1 carrot
- 1 medium onion
- 1 stalk celery
- 3 white mushrooms
- 100g/½ cup cherry tomatoes
- 1 garlic clove
- 15g/2 tbsp extra virgin olive oil
- 1 stalk rosemary
- 1 stalk oregano
- 10 dried capers (previously washed)
- Salt and pepper, to taste

Method

1. Start by heating the oil and brown the garlic for two minutes for flavour.

2. Remove the garlic

3. Add chopped tomatoes, celery, carrot and onion to the Whatever Pan and cook for 8-10 minutes on a low heat.

4. Add the mushrooms, capers, rosemary and oregano. Cover with a lid and cook for 15 minutes.

5. Cook the fillet of beef on the grill for 3 minutes per side.

6. Add the fillet to the vegetables and cook for another 10 minutes.

7. Serve hot, adding salt and pepper to taste.

Traditional Irish Stew

This traditional casserole is the perfect comfort food for a wintery day!

 120 Mins 🍽 Serves 4

Ingredients

- 2 tbsp vegetable oil
- 400g/14oz. mutton or lamb cutlets
- 1kg/2.2lb potatoes, peeled and cut into quarters
- 2 carrots, chopped
- 1 onion, chopped
- 2 leeks, chopped
- 2 tbsp plain flour
- 600ml/1 pint beef stock
- Salt and pepper to taste

Method

1. Heat the oil in the Whatever Pan and add the lamb pieces. Cook until brown all over. Set aside half of the lamb cutlets and the lamb cutlets' fat.

2. Add half of the potatoes, carrots, onion, leeks.

3. Cover with the remaining cooked lamb cutlets, potatoes, onion and leeks.

4. In another pan, fry the lamb cutlets' fat, add the flour and stir well. Cook on a gentle heat for 3 minutes.

5. Add the fat and flour mixture to the lamb and vegetables in the Whatever Pan. Pour in the beef stock.

6. Cover, and cook for 2 hours on medium heat.

7. Season with salt and pepper and serve!

The Perfect T-Bone Steak

The garlic butter mixture paired with a succulent T-Bone steak is simply divine.

 30 Mins Serves 4

Ingredients

- 1 T-Bone steak (the bigger the better!)
- 10 cloves of garlic
- A handful of fresh parsley
- A handful of fresh thyme
- A handful of fresh rosemary
- 8 cherry tomatoes on the vine
- 1 large potato
- Salt & pepper
- Paprika
- 400g/1 ¼ cups of butter
- Whisky
- Olive oil

Method

1. Take the potato and slice it lengthways into slices 0.5cm thick, drizzle with olive oil and then season with salt, pepper and paprika.

2. Place half of your measured butter in a pan and warm gently until melted, switch off heat, and allow to cool.

3. Peel and finely chop 6 of the garlic cloves along with the parsley. Place them in a bowl and mix together with salt pepper and the melted butter. Set mixture aside for later.

4. Place your Whatever Pan onto your stove, grill or fire to heat up.

5. Take your steak, season on both sides with salt and pepper and then place into the pan on its side to sear the thick strip of fat for 1-2 minutes.

6. Once the fat has some colour, place the steak flat in the pan and cook for 2-3 minutes. Then turn the steak over and pour in a little of the whisky. If cooking over a fire, tip the pan to allow the whisky to catch alight, and flambee the steak for 30 seconds.

7. Now, add the remaining butter and 4 garlic cloves to the pan along with the fresh rosemary and thyme. Cook for a further 2 minutes, basting the steak constantly with the melted butter and herbs. Then, take the steak out of the pan and allow it to rest.

8. While the steak is resting, place the sliced potatoes and cherry tomatoes into the pan. Fry the potatoes for 3 minutes on each side whilst allowing the skin to blister on the tomatoes.

9. Remove the potatoes and tomato from the pan. To serve, cut the steak from the bone and slice into thin strips. Place alongside the potatoes and tomatoes, and drizzle over a few spoons of the garlic and herb butter that was set aside earlier. Then enjoy!

"Make sure you preheat your Whatever Pan so that the steak sizzles when it touches the pan. If it's not hot enough, it will steam rather than getting the perfect sear."

—————————— Men With The Pot

Chicken Katsu Curry

This restaurant favourite is so simple to make at home. Our 30 minute recipe balances the rich sauce with a fresh and zingy vegetable salad.

 30 Mins Serves 1

Ingredients

- 1 skinless chicken breast
- 50g/⅓ cup flour
- 1 egg
- 100g/1 cup panko breadcrumbs
- 10ml/2 tsp olive oil

For the sauce

- 10ml/2 tsp oil
- 1 onion
- 2 garlic cloves, crushed
- 1 piece of fresh root ginger
- 5g/1tsp curry powder
- 10g/1 tbsp flour
- 500ml/17fl oz chicken stock
- 10ml/1.5 tsp honey
- 5ml/1 tsp soy sauce

For the garnish

- 150g/⅔ cups rocket (arugula)
- 1 peeled carrot
- 10g/1 tbsp parsley
- 5ml/1 tsp lime juice
- Salt to taste

Method

1. Place chicken between 2 pieces of clingfilm and bash with a rolling pin to flatten to about 1cm thick.

2. Place the egg and breadcrumbs in separate bowls. Then, dip the chicken breast in the egg and then in the breadcrumbs, ensuring each breast is coated well.

3. Heat oil in the Whatever Pan over a medium-high heat. When the oil is hot fry the coated breast for 3–4 minutes on each side, then transfer to a plate lined with kitchen paper to soak up any excess oil. Set aside and keep warm.

4. In a saucepan, add 10ml/2 tsp of oil and fry the onion, garlic, ginger. Then, add curry powder, flour, chicken stock, honey and soy sauce. Once cooked, set aside.

5. For the garnish just add rocket, carrot, parsley, lime juice, salt and mix well.

6. You can place the chicken breast on a bed of rice if preferred and pour the sauce onto it. Enjoy!

"Panko breadcrumbs are brilliant for extra crunchy fried chicken."

——————————— Chef Inocan Ákos

KFC Style
Fried Chicken

Want to recreate this iconic dish at home? Try our
recipe for delicious KFC Fried Chicken!

 30 Mins   Serves 4

Ingredients

- 1.5kg/3.3lb chicken legs
- 225g/1 cup buttermilk
- 1 large egg
- 120g/1 cup flour
- 5g/2 tsp chili powder
- 5g/2 tsp dried marjoram
- 5g/2 tsp ground oregano
- 5g/2 tsp dried sage
- 5g/2 tsp dried basil
- 5g/2 tsp onion salt
- 5g/2 tsp garlic powder
- 10g/1.5 tbsp paprika
- 10g/2 tsp salt

Method

1. Cut the chicken legs in half.
2. Add the buttermilk and the egg to a bowl and whisk well.
3. In another bowl, add flour and all spices and mix well.
4. Soak up the chicken in the buttermilk and egg. Then, dredge it in the flour mixture on all sides and shake off the excess coating.
5. Add oil to The Whatever Pan and heat it to 175°C/350°F degrees.
6. Add the chicken and fry for 8 minutes on each side.
7. Remove the chicken from the oil and add to a drying rack on top of a clean baking sheet. Voilà!

Chicken Lollipops

A delicious and fun dinner party meal

 35 Mins   Serves 4

Ingredients

- 8 chicken legs
- 10g/1.5 tbsp BBQ rub
- Salt to taste
- 10ml/2 tsp oil
- 5g/1 tsp butter
- 120g/½ cup BBQ sauce

Method

1. Preheat oven to 200°C/390°F.
2. Cut along the circumference of the thin end of the chicken legs and remove the excess meat.
3. Place the chicken legs in a large mixing bowl and add BBQ rub and salt, then mix well.
4. Add oil and butter to your Whatever Pan. Place your chicken legs in the pan and fry for 5 minutes, 2.5 minutes on each side.
5. Drizzle the BBQ sauce over the chicken legs and place in the oven for about 15 minutes. Take them out and serve!

RECOMMENDED PRODUCT

ORIENTAL CHEFS KNIVES

Marinated Peri-Peri Chicken Thighs and Drumsticks

This is how we cooked Peri-Peri chicken inspired by the likes of Nando's. If you have the ingredients, the Whatever Pan, 45 minutes and a good appetite - you're in luck.

 45 Mins   Serves 4

Ingredients

- 1kg/2.2lb of chicken thighs and drumsticks
- 3 cloves of garlic (minced)
- 15g/2.5 tbsp lemon zest
- Juice of 1 lemon
- 30g/2 tbsp orange juice
- 4 tbsp olive oil
- 7g/1.5 tsp sea salt
- 30g/1 oz sweet paprika
- 1/4 tsp black pepper
- 7g/3 tsp red pepper flakes
- 15g/2 tbsp oregano
- 15g/1 cube butter

Method

1. Add the chicken to a large mixing bowl.

2. Add oregano, lemon zest, garlic, sweet paprika, sea salt, red pepper flakes, lemon juice, orange juice and olive oil. Mix well and let marinate for 4 hours.

3. Pre-heat the oven to 200°C/390°F.

4. Preheat your Whatever Pan and once hot, add olive oil and butter.

5. Once the butter is melted and the skillet is hot, add the chicken skin side down and cook undisturbed on medium high heat for 4 minutes, or until chicken is nicely browned.

6. Flip chicken over (skin side up) and move the pan to the oven. Bake uncovered for 30 minutes at 200°C/390°F.

7. Remove from the oven, ensure that the chicken is cooked through and serve!

Chicken Fajitas

Here's a vibrant and simple midweek meal the whole family will love! Chicken Fajitas are simple to make and just delicious!

 35 Mins   Serves 4

Ingredients

- 115ml/½ cup olive oil
- 60ml/¼ cup lime juice
- 2 tsp cumin
- ½ tsp red pepper flakes
- 450g/1 lb chicken
- 1 large onion
- 3 bell peppers
- Salt and black pepper to taste
- Tortillas

Method

1. In a bowl add the olive oil, lime juice, cumin, and red pepper flakes and whisk well.

2. Add chicken breasts to the marinade and marinate for 2 hours in the fridge.

3. Heat up your Whatever Pan and add the chicken breasts. Cook the meat through, then set aside and cut into small pieces.

4. Throw the peppers in the pan and add the lime mixture and salt and pepper.

5. Add the chicken back in and cook with the peppers.

6. Once ready, grab a spoonful of the chicken and peppers, place it in a tortilla, and voilà!

RECOMMENDED PRODUCT

PLASTIC MIXING BOWLS

Pot-Roasted Chicken
with Smoked Bacon

Wrapping chicken with bacon elevates the meal by
adding flavour and ensuring it has a succulent texture.

 40 Mins — Serves 2

Ingredients

- 2 chicken legs with skin on
- 3 large mushrooms
- 1 large onion
- 1 red chilli
- 6 cloves of garlic
- 300g/10.5 oz of smoked bacon or pork belly
- Salt & pepper
- 4 tsp of paprika
- 1 tbsp of wholegrain mustard
- 1 tbsp of clear honey
- 330ml/11.5fl oz of beer (we prefer Lucky Saint)
- Fresh thyme
- Fresh parsley

Method

1. Place your Whatever Pan on your hob, grill or fire to heat up and pre-heat your oven to 180°C/350°F.
2. Chop the mushrooms in half, and slice the onion into rings, about 1 cm thick.
3. Roughly chop the garlic and chilli, then cut the bacon into long strips about 1cm thick.
4. Season the chicken legs with a generous amount of salt and pepper and half of the paprika.
5. Place the chicken legs and bacon strips into the Whatever Pan and begin to brown.
6. After 5 mins turn the chicken and bacon strips over. Then add the onion, garlic and mushrooms to the pan.
7. After a further 3 minutes, turn the mushrooms and onions over and cook for another 2 minutes.
8. Now that everything is nicely browned on both sides, pour in the beer and wait for it to simmer.
9. Add more salt and pepper and the remainder of the paprika to the pan, followed by the wholegrain mustard, fresh thyme, chilli and honey.
10. Place the lid on the pan and put into the oven for 20 minutes at 180°C/350°F.
11. Remove from the oven and allow to cool, then garnish with fresh parsley and serve.

Duck Legs in Beer

A rich, one-pan dinner for three, cooked slowly to give you thin, crispy skin and beautiful, melt-in-your-mouth meat.

 50 Mins — Serves 3

Ingredients

- 3 duck legs
- 210g/7 oz. chopped carrots
- 2 chopped onions
- 90g/3 oz. celery roots
- 4 sprigs of thyme
- 2 tbs. honey
- 420ml/15 oz. beer
- Salt & pepper to taste

Method

1. Place your duck legs in a pan and fry them for a few minutes until golden. Season them with salt and pepper, then set aside.
2. To your pan, add carrots, onions, celery roots, thyme and season with salt and pepper.
3. Fry for a few minutes and place your duck legs on top of the vegetables.
4. Finally, add the honey and beer, cook for 40 min and serve!

Caprese Stuffed Chicken

This Caprese Stuffed Chicken Recipe is an easy, healthy dish that will wow all your dinner guests.

 40 Mins   Serves 4

Ingredients

- 4 Boneless skinless chicken breasts
- 60g/2 cups baby spinach
- 54g/1 cup sun-dried tomatoes
- 4 mozzarella slices
- 1 ½ tbsp. Italian seasoning
- Salt and pepper to taste

Method

1. Preheat the oven to 200°C/400°F. On a clean work surface, cut a pocket into each chicken breast.
2. Stuff each chicken breast with baby spinach, sun-dried tomatoes, and 1 mozzarella slice.
3. Season with Italian seasoning, salt and pepper, and secure with toothpicks.
4. Heat olive oil in your Whatever Pan and sear your chicken breasts until golden, 3 minutes per side.
5. Transfer to the oven, cook for 15 minutes and voilà!

Spicy Parmesan Salmon

Love salmon? Add this crunchy, herby, cheesy recipe to your repertoire.

---

 25 Mins Serves 2

Ingredients

- 1 tbsp. olive oil
- 4 salmon fillets
- 2 tbsp. butter
- 3 cloves minced garlic
- Juice of 1 lemon
- 2 tbsp. Cajun seasoning
- 1 tbsp. chopped parsley
- 2 tbsp. grated Parmesan
- 4-5 lemon slices

Method

1. Heat the olive oil in your Whatever Pan and add the salmon fillets.
2. Turn fillets after a few minutes and cook with lid on for 5 minutes.
3. Remove salmon fillets and set aside.
4. Melt butter in the pan and add minced garlic.
5. Fry for a few minutes and add lemon juice, Cajun seasoning, parsley, and Parmesan.
6. Fry for a few minutes and add your salmon fillets. Spread some of the Parmesan mix onto the fillets and add 4-5 lemon slices to the pan.
7. Cook with lid on for 5 minutes and serve!

RECOMMENDED PRODUCT

ELECTRONIC SALT AND PEPPER MILL

Ginger Shrimp Toast

Top some sliced baguette with these lemony ginger shrimps - you won't be able to stop at 1!

 25 Mins Serves 4

Ingredients

- 140g/1 ⅓ cups shrimp/prawns
- 1tbsp ginger
- 1 baguette
- 2tbsp lemon juice
- 3tbsp sesame oil
- Sesame Seeds
- 3tbsp olive oil
- ½ tsp salt
- Pepper
- Butter
- Rocket/arugula

Method

1. Place the shrimp in a bowl, add ginger, lemon juice, salt, sesame oil, olive oil, pepper, mix well and let marinate for 15 minutes.

2. Slice the baguette diagonally into approximately 1-2cm slices; spread the butter over the slices and place in the Whatever Pan.

3. Heat over medium heat for a few minutes until butter is melted.

4. Remove the bread, place the shrimps in the pan and cook until the prawns turn pink.

5. Finally, put the bread slices on your plate, place some rocket salad on the slices, add the shrimp and sprinkle with sesame seeds.

Seared Asian style tuna steaks

These Asian style cooked tuna steak take only 10 minutes to make - they're healthy, crispy and seared on the outside, and medium-rare on the inside.

 10 Mins Serves 2

Ingredients

- 2 Tuna steaks
- 1 tbsp. olive oil
- 1 tbsp. honey
- 2 tbsp. soy sauce
- Sesame seeds, handful
- 1 green/spring onion, chopped
- 1 lime wedge
- Salt to taste

Method

1. Heat olive oil in your Whatever Pan over medium heat.

2. Then, add the tuna steaks with the honey, soy sauce, sesame seeds and salt.

3. Sear for 2 minutes each side and remove from heat. Allow to rest for at least 3 minutes.

4. Slice into 1/2-inch slices.

5. Serve garnished with green onions, toasted sesame seeds, and a squeeze of fresh lime juice.

RECOMMENDED PRODUCT

OVAL BAMBOO CHOPPING BOARD

Supergrain Salmon Salad

Get into the superfood revolution with this healthy combination of grilled salmon, farro, harissa and herbs, all mixed together in a deliciously spiced main course salad.

 40 Mins Serves 2

Ingredients

- 425g/15 oz salmon
- 200g/7 oz farro
- Vegetable stock (typically cubed)
- 2 tbsp harissa paste
- Olive oil
- 2 tbsp chopped mint leaves
- 2 tbsp lemon juice
- ⅓ tsp chilli powder
- 1 tsp ground cumin
- Bunch of salad leaves
- Salt and pepper, to taste

Method

1. Boil water in a saucepan and add salt and vegetable stock. Then, add the grains to the water and cook for about 30 minutes, (or until tender) then drain.

2. Place the salmon on a chopping board; add pepper to taste and brush generously with harissa paste.

3. Grill for 5-6 minutes, or until the salmon is cooked through.

4. Whilst the salmon is cooking, add olive oil, chopped mint leaves, lemon juice, chilli powder, and cumin to a bowl and mix well.

5. Cut your salmon into large chunks.

6. Pile the grains on salad leaves, add salmon chunks and add sauce.

7. Serve this deliciousness!

Chicken Seafood Paella

This colourful recipe has a bit of everything! It's wonderfully comforting and extremely flavoursome!

 80 Mins Serves 6

Ingredients

- 4 chicken thighs
- 1 onion, chopped
- 2 litres/8.5 cups chicken stock
- 500g/2.5 cups paella rice
- 1 heaped teaspoon smoked paprika
- 2 large pinches of saffron
- 2 handfuls of fresh or frozen peas
- 10 large raw shell-on king prawns
- 500g/1lb mussels
- Fresh thyme
- 1 lemon, quarters
- Himalayan salt, to taste
- Olive oil

Method

1. Heat some olive oil in your Whatever Pan and add Himalayan salt.

2. Start frying your chicken thighs until golden and crispy.

3. Add the onion, chicken stock, paella rice, paprika, saffron and leave to cook on a medium heat for around 20 minutes, stirring occasionally.

4. Add the peas, king prawns, mussels, and cook until rice is soft.

5. Add thyme and serve with wedges of lemon for squeezing over.

Grilled Octopus with Aubergine

Cooking octopus at home is much easier than you might think. Our simple recipe is sure to be a crowd pleaser.

 45 Mins — Serves 2

Ingredients

- 1 octopus (approx. 1kg/2.2lb)
- 1 courgette/zucchini
- 1 aubergine
- 100g/1 ¾ cups sun-dried tomatoes
- 100g/1 cup olives
- 1 garlic clove
- Mixed stalks (rosemary, sage, laurel)
- Extra virgin olive oil
- Salt and pepper, to taste

Method

1. Start by boiling the octopus in water previously flavoured with sprigs and garlic clove. Boil it for 30/35 minutes and then allow it to cool in the water.

2. Whilst it's boiling, cut the courgette and aubergine into wide slices, grill them, and then cut again into sticks.

3. Mix the courgette and aubergine sticks with the dried tomatoes and olives. Then add extra virgin olive oil, and salt and pepper to taste.

4. Cut the octopus into equal portions (approx. 2 legs per person)

5. Grill the octopus legs for 2 minutes, add the previously mixed vegetables and stir fry for 1 minute more.

> "You should always use frozen octopus because it is easier to cook and becomes very tender during the cooking process."

—————————— Chef Luca La Rosa

Shrimps with Mustard and Honey Sauce

Cooking shrimps with their shells on is not only visually pleasing, it will help them retain their delicious flavour.

 30 Mins Serves 2

Ingredients

- 10g/¾ tbsp extra virgin olive oil
- 25g/1.5 tbsp mustard
- 25g/1.5 tbsp mustard with seeds
- 25g/1.5 tbsp honey
- 4 whole prawns
- 50g/¼ cup cooked black rice
- Salt and pepper, to taste
- Pinch of smoked paprika

Method

1. Prepare the sauce by mixing the mustard, mustard with seeds and honey with a spoon. Then, leave to rest for 10 minutes.

2. Butterfly cut the prawns by cutting them on the back from the head to the tip of the tail, leaving the head intact.

3. De-vein the prawns.

4. Cook the prawns with a little olive oil starting from the back, 2 minutes per side.

5. When cooked, place the prawns on black rice and add the mustard and honey sauce with a little smoked paprika.

6. Add salt and pepper to taste.

> "As with all shellfish, you should cook this quickly over a high heat so the shrimps don't become rubbery."
>
> —————— Chef Luca La Rosa

White Fish Tagine

A super quick and deliciously healthy recipe!

 25 Mins Serves 2

Ingredients

- 1 tbsp vegetable oil
- 4 garlic cloves, chopped
- 250g/2 cups cherry tomatoes, halved
- 250g/2 cups asparagus, chopped
- 2 x 150g/5oz fish fillets
- 2 tbsp rose harissa
- Zest of 1 lemon
- Juice of ½ lemon
- 150ml/5fl. oz water
- Salt and pepper to taste

Method

1. Heat vegetable oil in your Whatever Pan and start frying your garlic, cherry tomatoes and asparagus. Season with salt and pepper.

2. Add the fish fillets and rub them with the harissa paste.

3. Finely grate the lemon zest over the fish, and squeeze over half the juice.

4. Add 150ml of water, cover and cook for 5 minutes, or until the fish is just cooked through.

5. Serve with a side of couscous.

RECOMMENDED PRODUCT

SILICONE BRUSH SET

Drunk Salmon

Cooking the salmon in whisky gives
it a wonderful smoky flavour.

 30 Mins · Serves 1

Ingredients

For the salad
- 1 tomato
- 1 cucumber
- Handful of lettuce
- 1 onion
- 1 block feta cheese

For the dressing
- 100ml/3.5fl. oz Whisky
- 2 tbsp olive oil
- 2 tbsp honey
- 1 tbsp wholegrain mustard
- Lemon juice, of half a lemon
- Salt and pepper, to taste
- Parsley, handful

For the salmon
- 1 salmon fillet
- Salt and pepper, to taste
- 1 lemon, sliced
- 200ml/7fl. oz Whisky

Method

1. Start by preparing your salad. Peel off the skin of the cucumber and chop into chunks along with the tomatoes.
2. Chop the lettuce and then the onion into very small pieces.
3. Chop the feta cheese into cubes 1 cm thick.
4. Add the chopped cucumber, tomatoes, lettuce, onion and feta into a large bowl.
5. For the dressing, add the whisky, olive oil, honey, wholegrain mustard, lemon juice, salt and pepper and parsley into a bowl and mix well. Pour over the salad and leave some aside to pour over the salmon later.
6. Place your Whatever Pan on your hob, grill or fire to heat up.
7. Drizzle the salmon fillet with olive oil and season with salt and pepper.
8. Cook the fillet skin side down until crispy. Remove the fillet from the Whatever Pan and place 9 slices of lemon in the pan.
9. Place the salmon fillet on top of the lemon slices, face down. Pour over the whisky and cook until the alcohol has evaporated for another 5-10 minutes.
10. Once the salmon is ready, put the salad onto a plate, and place the fillet on top.
11. Drizzle with the remaining dressing and serve.

Creamy Salmon with Sun-dried Tomatoes

Simple, healthy and on your table in 30 minutes. This creamly salmon is the perfect midweek (restaurant quality) supper.

 30 Mins Serves 4

Ingredients

- 4 Salmon Steaks
- 1 tbsp butter
- 480ml/2 cups cream
- 50g/1 cup sun-dried tomatoes
- 1 tbsp paprika
- 1 tbsp French mustard
- Salt to taste
- Parsley

Method

1. Fry the salmon steaks in your Whatever Pan for a few minutes per side.
2. Remove from the Whatever Pan and set aside.
3. Add butter and let it melt. Once melted add the cream, sun-dried tomatoes, paprika and mustard and season with salt.
4. Whisk or mix, then add the salmon steaks and the parsley.
5. Cook with lid on for approximately 10 minutes and voilà!

Blackened Roast Salmon

Use punchy spices to flavour this salmon dish. This healthy dish will definitely not disappoint!

 30 Mins  Serves 2

Ingredients

- 3 tbsp. olive oil
- 2 salmon fillets
- 3 bell peppers, cut into chunks
- 2 red onions, peeled and cut into wedges
- 1 garlic clove, crushed
- ½ tsp. cayenne pepper
- 1 tbsp. brown sugar
- 1 tsp. dried oregano
- 400g/1 can red beans
- 2 limes, zested and juiced
- Salt, to taste

Method

1. Heat olive oil in your frying pan and start frying the bell peppers and onion.
2. Meanwhile in a small bowl, mix the garlic, brown sugar, cayenne pepper, oregano and salt.
3. Add it to your vegetables and sauté for a few minutes.
4. Add the red beans and the lime zest and fry until cooked through. Set aside.
5. In your Whatever Pan, add salt and olive oil and start frying the salmon fillets.
6. Add the lime juice and the vegetable mixture and fry until the salmon is cooked through.
7. Serve and enjoy!

Chickpea Salad with Sundried Tomatoes and Halloumi

A quick salad for two with nutty chickpeas, golden grilled halloumi, and a gentle vinegar tang. Best served with good fresh bread to mop up the juices.

 20 Mins Serves 2

Ingredients

- 1 onion
- 800g/4 cups tinned chickpeas
- 4-6 sun-dried tomatoes, chopped
- Handful of parsley
- 60ml/4 tbsp extra virgin olive oil
- 15g/1 tbsp whole grain mustard
- 15ml/3 tsp red wine vinegar
- 15ml/3 tsp white wine vinegar
- 15ml/3 tsp lemon juice
- 150g/1 cup halloumi

Method

1. Finely chop the onion and parsley using a fine knife.

2. Mix the chickpeas, onion, tomatoes and parsley together.

3. In a small bowl, mix the olive oil, vinegars, lemon juice and mustard.

4. Grill the halloumi in your Whatever Pan until brown on each side.

5. Crumble the halloumi over the salad, pour over the dressing and serve.

RECOMMENDED PRODUCT

CHOPAHOLIC ESSENTIAL KITCHEN KNIVES

Family Frittata

A completely satisfying one-pan meal, this frittata is just as delicious served warm or at room temperature.

 45 Mins Serves 4

Ingredients

- 360g/13 oz potatoes
- 1 onion
- 1 red pepper
- 1 courgette
- 6 eggs
- 30g/⅓ cup parmesan
- 1 pinch paprika
- Salt to taste

Method

1. Boil the potatoes for 10 minutes.
2. Fry the onion gently in a little olive oil until soft.
3. Add the red pepper and courgette and continue to cook gently.
4. When the pepper and courgette are soft, add the potatoes.
5. In a large mixing bowl, lightly beat the eggs together with the parmesan, paprika and salt.
6. Add the egg mix to the vegetables.
7. Place the Whatever Pan in the oven for approximately 30 minutes at 190°C/370°F.
8. Finish off under a hot grill.

"The Parmesan adds a sharp, nutty flavour but if you want your frittata to ooze with extra cheese, feel free to mix in some cheddar or gruyère".

——————— Chef Layla Powell

Courgette & Quinoa Stuffed Peppers

Take just 5 ingredients and create this super healthy, low-calorie, low-fat Mediterranean-style vegetarian bake

---

 30 Mins   Serves 4

Ingredients

- 4 red peppers
- 1 courgette/zucchini, quartered lengthwise and thinly sliced
- 2 x 250g packs ready-to-eat quinoa (3 cups in total)
- 85g/3oz feta cheese, finely crumbled
- Handful parsley, roughly chopped

Method

1. Heat oven to 180°C/350°F. Cut each pepper in half through the stem and remove the seeds.

2. Place the pepper halves on your Whatever Pan, drizzle with 1 tbsp olive oil and season with salt and pepper.

3. Place in the oven for 15 minutes.

4. Meanwhile, start frying your courgette in a frying pan and cook until soft. Remove from the heat, then stir in a bowl with the quinoa, feta and parsley. Season with pepper.

5. Remove the peppers from the oven and divide the quinoa mixture between the pepper halves, then return to the oven for 5 minutes to heat through.

Stuffed Butternut Squash

For all the veggie lovers out there - here's a recipe you could prepare for Christmas to impress all your guests. Packed with nuts and herbs, it definitely has plenty of flavour!

 80 Mins Serves 2

Ingredients

- 1 large butternut squash
- 1 tbsp. olive oil
- 1 onion, chopped
- 1 garlic, crushed
- 2 tbsp. pine nuts
- 2 tbsp. almond flakes
- 32g/¼ cup dried cranberries
- 60ml/⅓ cup vegetable stock
- 1 tsp. fennel seeds
- 2 tsp. Sage
- 50g/⅓ cup feta cheese
- Salt, to taste

Method

1. Heat oven to 180°C/350°F.

2. Cut the squash in half lengthways. Scoop out and discard the seeds and any fibrous bits.

3. Carve out a channel down the centre of both squash halves for stuffing. The squash shell should be about 1.5cm thick all over when you've finished. Set aside the squash interior.

4. Add olive oil to a frying pan and start cooking your onion and garlic for 5 minutes.

5. Add the pine nuts, almond flakes, dried cranberries, vegetable stock and the rest of your squash interior. Season with fennel seeds, sage, salt and feta.

6. Once cooked, pack the filling into the holes of the 2 squash halves. Tie the halves back together with long toothpicks.

7. Place in the oven for 1 hour and serve!

Oven Baked Red Pepper Risotto

An extremely easy, healthy and vegetarian risotto recipe!

---

35 Mins Serves 4

Ingredients

- 2 tbsp vegetable oil
- 1 onion, chopped
- 300g/1.5 cups risotto rice
- 100ml/3.4fl. oz white wine (optional, or use more stock)
- 400g/1 can chopped tomatoes
- 200g/1 ⅓ cups roasted peppers
- 500ml/17.5fl. oz vegetable stock
- Salt and pepper, to taste
- Parsley, to taste
- Parmesan, (optional)

Method

1. Preheat oven to 200°C/390°F.

2. Heat the oil in your Whatever Pan, then fry the onion for a few mins until softened.

3. Turn up the heat, tip in the rice, stir, then fry for 1 minute more.

4. Pour in the chopped tomatoes, roasted peppers, vegetable stock and white wine.

5. Cover and bake in the oven for 25 minutes until the rice is tender and creamy.

6. Once ready, season with salt, pepper, parsley and parmesan.

RECOMMENDED PRODUCT

BAMBOO SLOTTED SPATULA

Ratatouille

Enjoy this super-healthy classic French vegetarian dish, which counts as four of your five-a-day!

 80 Mins  Serves 6

Ingredients

- 2 aubergines/eggplants
- 2 courgettes/zucchini
- 1 squash
- 6 roma tomatoes

Sauce
- 2 tablespoons olive oil
- 1 onion, diced
- 4 cloves garlic, minced
- ½ red bell pepper, diced
- ½ yellow bell pepper, diced
- ½ green bell pepper, diced
- salt, to taste
- pepper, to taste
- 795g/28 oz can of crushed tomatoes
- 2 teaspoons chopped fresh parsley

Herb seasoning
- 2 tablespoons chopped fresh basil, from 8-10 leaves
- 2 tablespoons chopped fresh oregano
- 2 teaspoons fresh thyme
- Salt and pepper, to taste
- 4 tablespoons olive oil
- 1 teaspoon garlic, minced

Method

1. Preheat the oven for 170°C/350°F.

2. Slice the aubergines, tomatoes, squash, and courgettes into approximately 1 mm rounds, then set aside.

3. To make the sauce, heat the olive oil in your Whatever Pan over medium-high heat.

4. Sauté the onion, garlic, and bell peppers until soft, for about 10 minutes.

5. Season with salt and pepper, then add the crushed tomatoes. Stir until the ingredients are fully incorporated. Remove from heat, then add the parsley. Stir once more, then smooth the surface of the sauce with a spatula.

6. Arrange the sliced veggies in alternating patterns on top of the sauce from the outer edge to the middle of the pan.

7. To make the herb seasoning, mix together the parsley, oregano, thyme, salt, pepper, olive oil and garlic in a small bowl. Spoon the herb seasoning over the vegetables.

8. Place in the oven at 170°C/350°F and bake for 40 minutes.

Spicy Mexican Eggs

A delicious and flavoursome brunch recipe

 35 Mins 🛎 Serves 4

Ingredients

- 1 tbsp vegetable oil
- 1 red onion, cut into small chunks
- 3 garlic cloves, cut into small pieces
- Chili peppers, to taste
- Salt and pepper, to taste
- Cumin, to taste
- 400g/1 can of tomatoes
- 400g/1 can of red beans
- 4 tortillas
- 4 eggs
- Cheddar cheese, to taste

Method

1. Preheat oven to 180°C/350°F.
2. Add vegetable oil to your Whatever Pan and start frying the onion, garlic and chili peppers.
3. Season with salt, pepper and cumin. Fry for about 6-7 minutes.
4. Add the tomatoes and red beans and cook for approximately 7-10 minutes. Set aside.
5. Wash your whatever pan. Add vegetable oil, salt and pepper and lay the tortillas in the pan.
6. Add the tomatoes and beans mixture.
7. Crack the eggs in it and sprinkle with cheese.
8. Place in the oven for 20 minutes and serve.

Tuscan White Bean Skillet

A vegetarian Tuscan White Bean Skillet recipe made from pantry staples for a quick and delicious meal!

 30 Mins Serves 4

Ingredients

- 1 tbsp olive oil
- 125g/8 oz brown mushrooms
- 175g/1 ½ cups yellow onion
- 3 cloves garlic
- 40g/⅔ cups sun dried tomatoes
- 800g/2 cans diced tomatoes
- 400g/1 can cannellini beans
- 200g/12 ounces artichoke hearts
- ½ tsp dried thyme
- 1 tsp dried oregano
- Salt and pepper to taste
- Parsley for garnish

Method

1. Heat olive oil in the Whatever Pan and start sautéing the mushrooms, onion and garlic for about 5 minutes.

2. Add the sun dried tomatoes, diced tomatoes and cannellini beans. Cook until fragrant and softened.

3. Add the artichokes, salt and pepper, thyme and oregano. Turn the heat down and let cook for about 10 minutes.

4. Garnish with chopped parsley and serve with plenty of crusty bread.

Vegetarian Moussaka

The perfect comfort food every veggie needs in their life!

 60 Mins  Serves 6

Ingredients

- 1 tbsp olive oil
- 1 onion, finely chopped
- 1 tsp thyme
- 1 tsp oregano
- ½ tsp cinnamon
- 1 tbsp tomato puree
- 400g/1 can chopped tomatoes
- 1 vegetable stock cube
- 160g/5.5oz red lentils
- 2 large aubergines/ eggplants
- 2 potatoes
- 250g/1 cup ricotta cheese
- 50g/¼ cup cheddar cheese
- Parsley for garnish

Method

1. Preheat oven to 200°C/390°F.
2. Put the lentils into a bowl. Cover with water and set aside to soak.
3. Boil the potatoes for 15-20 minutes and until tender.
4. Heat olive oil in your Whatever Pan, add the onion and cook over medium heat until soft. Add the thyme, oregano, cinnamon and cook for 1 minute. Stir in the tomato puree, chopped tomatoes and vegetable stock.
5. Drain the lentils and stir into the tomato sauce, bring to the boil and simmer for around 20 minutes over medium heat, stirring occasionally until the lentils are soft. Remove from the pan and set aside. Wash the Whatever Pan.
6. Meanwhile, drain the potatoes. Scrape the skin off of the potatoes, then cut into thick slices.
7. Heat the Whatever Pan until hot then griddle the aubergine in batches until browned and softened and set aside.
8. Spoon half the lentil sauce into the pan, then layer half the potatoes and aubergines over the top. Top with the remaining lentils, potatoes and aubergines.
9. In a bowl, mix the ricotta and grated cheddar and spoon the mixture over the aubergines. Smooth out with a spatula to cover the top.
10. Bake in the oven for 25 minutes, or until golden brown.
11. Garnish with parsley and serve!

Spinach and Ricotta Cannelloni

An extremely easy, healthy and vegetarian risotto recipe!

🕐 75 Mins 🍽 Serves 6

Ingredients

- 280g/2.5 cups cannelloni
- 260g/2 cups baby leaf spinach
- 250g/1 cup ricotta cheese
- 250g/1 cup Greek yogurt
- ¼ tsp freshly grated nutmeg
- 1 garlic clove, crushed
- 1 lemon zest
- 690g/1 jar tomato and parmesan passata
- 70g/⅔ cup dried breadcrumbs

Method

1. Boil the cannelloni until al dente and set aside.

2. Heat the oven to 200°C/390°F. Add olive oil to your Whatever Pan and start frying the spinach. Once cooked, drain the water and add ricotta, Greek yogurt, nutmeg, garlic, lemon zest, salt and pepper.

3. Once the mixture is done fill the cannelloni and set aside.

4. Add tomato passata to the Whatever Pan, then add the cannelloni and cover with the rest of the passata.

5. Cover with foil and place in the oven for 30 minutes.

6. Remove the foil, sprinkle the breadcrumbs and bake for another 10 minutes.

RECOMMENDED PRODUCT

STAINLESS STEEL FOUR-SIDED GRATER

Chicken, Kale and Mushroom Pot Pie

A deliciously creamy dish for all the savoury
pie lovers!

 60 Mins   Serves 6

Ingredients

- 1 tbsp olive oil
- 1 large onion, finely chopped
- 3 thyme sprigs, leaves picked
- 2 garlic cloves, crushed
- 350g/12 oz chicken breasts, cut into small chunks
- 250g/2 cups chestnut mushrooms, sliced
- 300ml/10.5fl. oz chicken stock
- 100g/7 tbsp crème fraiche
- 1 tbsp wholegrain mustard
- 100g/3 oz kale
- 2 tsp cornflour, mixed with 1 tbsp cold water
- 375g/14 oz pack puff pastry, rolled into a circle slightly bigger than your dish
- 1 egg yolk, to glaze

Method

1. Heat oven to 200°C/390°F.

2. Heat ½ tbsp oil in your Whatever Pan. Add the onion and cook for 5 minutes. Sprinkle over the thyme and garlic and stir for 1 minute.

3. Turn up the heat and add the chicken and fry until golden. Add the mushrooms and the remaining oil.

4. Add the stock, crème fraîche, mustard and kale then season well. Add the cornflour mixture and stir.

5. Remove from the heat and cover with the puff pastry lid, pressing into the sides of the casserole dish. Slice a cross in the centre and glaze with the egg yolk.

6. Bake for 30 minutes until the pastry is puffed up and golden and voilà!

One Skillet Lasagna

Classic flavors and cheesy layers, this
is definitely a kid-friendly recipe!

 60 Mins Serves 6

Ingredients

- 340g/¾ lb ground beef
- 2 garlic cloves, crushed
- 400g/1 can diced tomatoes with basil, oregano and garlic
- 1 jar/can of spaghetti sauce (passata)
- 150ml/⅔ cup condensed cream of onion soup
- 2 eggs, beaten
- 280g/1 ¼ cups cottage cheese
- 1tbsp tomato puree
- 1 tsp. Italian seasoning
- Pack of no-cook lasagne noodles, soaked in water
- 225g/1 cup shredded mozzarella
- Salt and pepper, to taste

Method

1. Heat the oven to 190°C/375°F.

2. In your Whatever Pan, cook the ground beef and garlic over medium heat until meat is no longer pink. Add salt and pepper to taste.

3. Stir in tomatoes and spaghetti sauce and heat through. Transfer to a large bowl.

4. Meanwhile, in a small bowl, combine the onion soup, eggs, cottage cheese, tomato puree and Italian seasoning.

5. Spread your lasagne noodles in your Whatever Pan, add the tomato and meat sauce and spread evenly.

6. Add a layer of cottage cheese mixture and another layer of lasagne noodles. Repeat.

7. Cover with mozzarella and place in the preheated oven for 30 minutes.

8. Remove from oven, let cool for 5 minutes and serve.

Sweet Potato Parcel

Bake this sweet potato parcel as a vegan Christmas Day centrepiece, enhanced with the delicious flavours of sage and chestnuts!

 80 Mins   Serves 6

Ingredients

- 3 sweet potatoes, peeled and cut into 2-3cm chunks
- 5 tbsp cold pressed rapeseed oil
- 1 onion, thinly sliced
- 2 large garlic cloves, crushed
- Chili flakes, to taste
- 1 tsp sage
- 200g/1.5 cups chestnuts, roughly chopped
- 4 tbsp cranberry sauce
- 2 sheets filo pastry

Method

1. Heat oven to 180°C/350°F. Put the potatoes on a baking tray and toss with 1 tbsp of the oil. Season and roast for 25 minutes.

2. While the potatoes roast, heat some olive oil in your Whatever Pan and add the onion and garlic. Season with sage and chili flakes and cook over a medium heat for about 7-10 minutes.

3. Add the chestnuts, cranberry sauce and the sweet potato cubes. Set the mix aside after cooking for a couple of minutes.

4. Clean the Whatever Pan.

5. Cover the Whatever Pan with 1 sheet of Filo Pastry.

6. Spoon the sweet potato mixture into the Whatever Pan and cut of any excess pastry.

7. Cover with another sheet of Filo pastry. Carefully fold the edges and brush with some olive oil.

8. Place in the oven and bake for 30 minutes, and voilà!

Savoury Dutch
Baby Pancake

The alternative pancake - a perfect brunch
recipe. Savour it baby!

 30 Mins   Serves 2

Ingredients

For the batter
- 3 eggs
- 2 tbsp unsalted butter
- 180ml/¾ cup whole milk
- 70g/½ cup all-purpose flour
- 2 tbsp corn-starch
- Salt & pepper to taste
- 1 tbsp butter (to melt)

Toppings
- 1 egg
- ½ avocado
- 2-3 slices of ham

Method

1. Preheat the oven to 220°C/420°F.

2. In a blender add 3 eggs, butter, milk, all-purpose flour, corn-starch, salt and pepper and blend until frothy.

3. Melt 1 tbsp of butter in the Whatever Pan and once hot, add your batter.

4. Place the Whatever Pan in the preheated oven and bake for 20 minutes until the batter is puffed and brown around the edges. It will begin to deflate as soon as it comes out.

5. Top with an egg, avocado and ham slices (you can also use other preferred toppings such bacon or salmon and crème fraîche).

RECOMMENDED PRODUCT

STONETASTIC
GRANITE
NON-STICK
FRYING PANS

Steak and Ale Pie

Good meat, good beer and good pastry - this steak and ale pie is definitely a winner.

 120 Mins Serves 6

Ingredients

For the pastry
- 225g/1.5 cups plain flour, plus extra for rolling out
- 1 tsp salt
- 8 tbsp/1 stick butter
- 150ml/5fl. oz water
- 1 egg yolk, beaten, to glaze

For the filling
- 600g/21 oz braising steak, cut into thick pieces
- 1 tbsp plain flour
- 300ml/10.5fl. oz brown ale
- 1 onion, roughly chopped
- 2 carrots, roughly chopped
- 2 sticks celery, roughly chopped
- 300ml/10fl. oz beef stock
- 400g/4 cups white mushrooms, halved or cut into quarters
- Knob of butter
- Salt, to taste

Method

1. For the pastry, mix the flour, salt, butter and water in large mixing bowl until it becomes a rough dough.

2. Gather the dough in the bowl, then turn it onto a work surface. Squash the dough into a fat, flat sausage, without kneading. Wrap in cling film then chill in the fridge for 15 minutes.

3. Lightly flour the work surface and the pastry.

4. Roll out the pastry in one direction until it's 1cm/0.4in thick and three times as long as it is wide.

5. Turn the dough so that its open edge is facing the right, like a book. Press the edges of the pastry together using your rolling pin.

6. Roll out and fold the pastry again, repeating about four times to make a smooth dough. If the pastry feels greasy at any point, or starts to spring back as you roll, cover and chill it for 10 minutes before continuing.

7. Meanwhile, lightly flour the steak chunks, add salt to taste and start braising them in your Whatever Pan. Cook for about 10 minutes.

8. Add 150 ml of brown ale and cook until golden-brown. Set aside.

9. Fry the onion, carrots, and celery. Pour in the stock and brown ale. Add the mushrooms.

10. Bring to the boil, cover and simmer for 1–1½ hours until the beef is tender, and the sauce has thickened. Set aside to cool.

11. To make the pie, preheat the oven to 200°C/390°F. Flour the work surface, then roll out the pastry to 6mm/0.22in thickness and wide enough to cover your Whatever Pan. Make sure you have 1 part to layer the Whatever Pan and 1 part to cover the mixture.

12. Butter the Whatever Pan and place your pastry inside it. Add the beef mixture and cover with the layer of pastry.

13. Brush the top with a little egg yolk and place in the oven for 10 minutes.

Grill Pan Waffles

There's no need to buy a waffle maker if you have a griddle pan (or our Whatever Pan)! These crispy, light, golden-brown waffles are perfect for a breakfast or teatime treat.

 15 Mins  Serves 2

Ingredients

- 120ml/4fl. oz full fat milk
- 120ml/4fl. oz cream
- 1 egg
- 15g/1.5 tbsp caster sugar
- 150g/1 cup flour
- 15g/1 tbsp baking powder
- 60ml/4 tbsp melted butter
- Whipped cream
- Maple syrup
- Handful of nuts
- Toppings of your choice!

Method

1. Whisk together the milk, cream, egg, caster sugar and flour and add melted butter.

2. Heat your Whatever Pan over high heat.

3. Whilst it's heating up, rub a block of butter all over the ridges where you will be dropping your batter.

4. Once the Frying pan is hot, turn down the heat to medium-low and add a spoonful of batter to the pan.

5. Cook the waffle for approximately 3 minutes per each side.

6. Once all waffles are done, serve with maple syrup and whipped cream or toppings of your choice.

RECOMMENDED PRODUCT

DIGITAL KITCHEN SCALES

Caramel-Pecan Cheesecake

Whilst it seems complicated to bake, this nutty, rich and delicious pecan cheesecake recipe is a snap to make and perfect for fall!

 60 Mins Serves 6

Ingredients

- 1 sheet pie crust
- 1 package cream cheese (225g/8oz), softened
- 150g/1 cup sugar
- 4 large eggs, room temperature
- 1 teaspoon vanilla extract
- 115g/1 cup chopped pecans
- 1 tub caramel ice cream topping

Method

1. Preheat the oven to 180°C/350°F.

2. Line your Whatever Pan with the pie crust. Trim and flute edges.

3. In a small bowl, beat cream cheese, sugar, 1 egg and vanilla until smooth.

4. Spread into crust and sprinkle with pecans.

5. In a small bowl, whisk the remaining eggs and gradually whisk in caramel topping until blended.

6. Pour slowly over pecans.

7. Bake for 35-40 minutes or until lightly browned. Then leave it to cool down for 2-3 hours and serve!

Strawberry Skillet Pie

A deliciously gooey and summery dessert recipe that will most definitely please everyone in the family

 120 Mins 🍽 Serves 6

Ingredients

For the crust
- 170g/1 ¼ cups plain flour
- 1 tbsp sugar
- ½ tbsp salt
- 8 tbsp/1 stick cold butter
- 3 tbsp water

For the filling
- 1.13kg/2 ½ lbs strawberries
- 340g/1 ½ cups sugar
- 3 tbsp quick cooking tapioca
- 85g/1 cup rolled oats
- 70g/½ cup flour
- 100g/½ cup sugar
- 8 tbsp/1 stick cold butter

Method

1. Preheat oven to 170°C/340°F.
2. For the crust, mix flour, sugar, salt, butter, water and using your hands until it forms a uniform ball.
3. Lay it out on a floured surface with a rolling pin.
4. Butter your Whatever Pan and place the crust on top of it.
5. For the filling, mix the strawberries, sugar, and tapioca in a bowl and add the filling on top of the crust in your pan.
6. In a separate bowl mix the oats, flour, sugar and butter until it becomes a paste and place on top of the strawberry mix.
7. Place in the oven for 1 ½ hours and serve!

Shoofly Chocolate Pie

Shoofly Chocolate Pie - an easy, full flavoured Pennsylvania Dutch recipe, and no mixer required!

 80 Mins Serves 6

Ingredients

- Pastry for single-crust pie
- 80g/½ cup semisweet chocolate chips
- 200g/1 ½ cups all-purpose flour
- 60g/½ cup brown sugar
- 3 tbsp butter or butter-flavoured shortening
- 1 tsp baking soda
- 350ml/1 ½ cups water
- 1 egg
- 280g/1 cup molasses

Method

1. Preheat oven to 220°C/425°F.

2. Roll out dough to fit in your Whatever Pan. Trim to 2-3 cm beyond the rim of the pan and flute the edges.

3. Sprinkle chocolate chips into the crust and set aside.

4. Meanwhile, in a bowl, combine all-purpose flour, brown sugar and butter until crumbly. Set 1 cup aside for topping.

5. Add the baking soda, egg, molasses and water and mix well.

6. Pour over the chocolate chips and sprinkle with the remaining crumb mixture.

7. Bake for 50 minutes and let it stand for 15 minutes before cutting.

Lemon Coconut Swirl Skillet Danish

Who doesn't love a good Danish pastry? This recipe is deliciously gooey and will disappear in a heartbeat!

 120 Mins  Serves 6

Ingredients

For Danish
- 4 tbsp butter, softened
- 112g/4oz cream cheese, softened
- 55g/¼ cup brown sugar
- 55g/¼ cup Sugar
- 1 lemon zest
- 50g/½ cup shredded coconut
- 450g/1lb store bought pizza dough

For Cream Cheese Icing
- 170g/1 ½ cup powdered sugar
- 60ml/¼ cup milk
- 1 tsp vanilla
- 112g/4oz cream cheese, softened

Method

1. Preheat the oven to 170°C/340°F.
2. Grease the bottom and sides of your Whatever Pan with butter.
3. In a bowl, stir together cream cheese and softened butter until smooth.
4. In another bowl stir together brown sugar, sugar, and lemon zest.
5. Roll the dough into a 14 inch square.
6. Spread the dough with cream cheese mixture on one half, and sprinkle sugar mixture on the other half.
7. Sprinkle the coconut over the half with the cream cheese mixture.
8. Fold the half with the shredded coconut over the half with sugar and press lightly to adhere.
9. Cut the dough lengthwise into 4-5 strips. Tightly twist each dough strip.
10. Starting in the centre of the greased Whatever Pan, wrap strips in a spiral pattern, pinching ends together. Cover and let stand in a warm place for about 30 minutes. After 30 minutes, place in the oven and bake for 30 minutes.
11. Meanwhile, prepare the cream cheese icing. In a bowl, stir together the powdered sugar, milk, vanilla extract, and cream cheese until smooth.
12. Once the dough is ready, drizzle with the cream cheese icing and serve warm.

Caring for your Whatever Pan

Using your Whatever Pan

- The Whatever Pan works on any hob/stovetop including gas, induction, ceramic, electric or Aga.
- The Whatever Pan is built to work just as beautifully inside your oven as on your stove, and is suitable for temperatures up to 250°C / 482°F. The lid is suitable for oven use up to 180°C / 350°F.
- Avoid metal utensils. Although Jean Patrique cast aluminium is very durable, it is best practice to use wood, plastic or silicone utensils instead of metal.

Cleaning your Whatever Pan

- Always let your pan cool completely before cleaning. Washing a hot pan in cold water can cause the metal to irreversibly warp because of the sudden changes in temperature.
- Only use non-abrasive cleaners and sponges to avoid scratches.
- Always hand wash your pan and avoid using a dishwasher to protect it from discolouration and potentially diminishing its non-stick properties.
- To remove stubborn food residue, soak your pan in warm, soapy water for a few hours before gently scrubbing.
- To remove minor stains or water spots, wipe your pan with vinegar or lemon juice and then rinse with water.